PEOPLES OF THE
ANCIENT WORLD

# Life of the
# Ancient
# Vikings

## Hazel Richardson

Crabtree Publishing Company
www.crabtreebooks.com

# Crabtree Publishing Company
www.crabtreebooks.com

## For Eben, Oliver, and Thomas

Coordinating editor: Ellen Rodger
Project Editor: Adrianna Morganelli
Editors: Rachel Eagen, Carrie Gleason
Production coordinator: Rosie Gowsell
Production assistance: Samara Parent
Scanning technician: Arlene Arch-Wilson
Art director: Rob MacGregor

Project management:
International Book Productions, Inc.:
Barbara Hopkinson
Judy Phillips
J. David Ellis
Dietmar Kokemohr
Sheila Hall

Consultant: Dr. Paul Cavill, Principal Research Fellow in the Institute for Name-Studies, University of Nottingham

Photographs: Brian and Cherry Alexander Photography/ Almay: p. 21 (top); Peter Anderson/ Dorling Kindersley: p. 22 (bottom); Art Archive: p. 12; Bettmann/ Corbis: p. 9 (bottom); Andy Crawford/ Dorling Kindersley: p. 11, p. 14 (top), p. 25; Richard Cummins/ Lonely Planet Images: p. 31 (top); Dorling Kindersley: p. 16 (right); Werner Forman/ Art Resource, NY: p. 14 (bottom), p. 16 (left), p. 18 (right); Werner Forman/ Corbis: p. 19 (top), p. 31 (bottom); Christopher J. Hall; Eye Ubiquitous/ Corbis: p. 7 (bottom); HIP/ Art resource, NY: p. 15; Archivo Iconografico, S.A./ Corbis: p. 3; Bob Krist/ Corbis: p. 4-5; Chis Lisle/ Corbis: p. 19 (bottom), p. 23; Courtesy Randolph Markham: p. 21 (top left); Jeff Mitchell/ Reuters/ Corbis: p. 30; Parks Canada: p. 8; Private Collection, Archives Charmet/ Bridgeman Art Library: p. 28; Scala/ Art Resource, NY: p. 9 (top); Stapleton Collection/ Corbis: p. 29 (top); Nik Wheeler/ Corbis: cover; Alan Witschonle Illustration: p. 29 (bottom); Christopher Wood Gallery, London, UK: p. 7 (top); York Archaeological Trust: p. 22 (right), p. 24

Illustrations: William Band: borders, pp. 4–5 (timeline), p .6 (map), p. 10, p. 13, p. 17, p. 20, p. 23 (top), pp. 26–27

Cover: A statue of Viking explorer, Leif Erikson, in Reykjavik, Iceland.

Contents: The Vikings were known for their detailed wooden carvings, such as this detail from a church door showing Siegfried slaying the dragon, Fafnir, from Hyllestad, Norway.

Title page: The Vikings were a seafaring people who built sturdy ships and traveled across oceans.

## Crabtree Publishing Company

www.crabtreebooks.com          1-800-387-7650

Cataloging-in-Publication Data
Richardson, Hazel.
   Life of the ancient Vikings / written by Hazel Richardson.
      p. cm. -- (Peoples of the ancient world)
   Includes index.
   ISBN-13: 978-0-7787-2044-7 (rlb)
   ISBN-10: 0-7787-2044-6 (rlb)
   ISBN-13: 978-0-7787-2074-4 (pbk)
   ISBN-10: 0-7787-2074-8 (pbk)
   1. Vikings--Juvenile literature. 2. Civilization, Viking--Juvenile literature. I. Title. II. Series.
   DL65.R54 2005
   948'.022--dc22
                                          2005001098
                                             LC

**Published in the United States**
PMB 16A
350 Fifth Ave.
Suite 3308
New York, NY
10118

**Published in Canada**
616 Welland Ave.
St. Catharines
Ontario, Canada
L2M 5V6

**Published in the United Kingdom**
73 Lime Walk
Headington
Oxford
0X3 7AD
United Kingdom

**Published in Australia**
386 Mt. Alexander Rd.
Ascot Vale (Melbourne)
V1C 3032

# Contents

# Sea Explorers

**The Vikings were fierce warriors who were feared for their daring and deadly raids on cities and towns across Europe. They were also the greatest explorers and traders of their time, and settled in lands far from their home countries.**

## Masters of the Northern Seas

The Vikings, also known as Norsemen, lived in the northern European countries of Norway, Sweden, and Denmark. Historians believe that their name may have come from the Norse word "vikingr," meaning pirate, or from "vik," meaning bay or harbor. The Vikings sailed large wooden ships, called longships, across oceans in search of new lands. They discovered Iceland and Greenland, and explored as far as North America hundreds of years before other Europeans knew it existed.

▶ *Northern Europe had a cold climate and little farmland, so the Vikings were forced to search for new land on which to grow food.*

| Vikings begin to raid England | Vikings start making silver coins | Vikings discover Iceland |
|---|---|---|
| 787 A.D. | 870 A.D. | 860 A.D. |

▼ *Stone carving shows a Viking attack on England at Lindisfarne Abbey.*

*Viking coins from England*

▼ *Iceland was discovered by Naddodd, a Viking from Norway.*

## Founders of the Modern World

The Vikings developed the economies of many European countries by building large trading towns across Europe. Viking traders were able to reach the trading towns by traveling over land on trade routes that stretched from modern-day Russia to China. The Vikings also founded many major cities, including Dublin in Ireland, Kiev in Ukraine, and Sicily in Italy.

# What is a "civilization?"

Most historians agree that a civilization is a group of people that shares common languages, some form of writing, advanced technology and science, and systems of government and religion.

The Viking territory of Danelaw, in England, founded in 886 A.D.

Erik the Red discovers Greenland in 982 A.D.

▾ *Erik the Red was an expert navigator and explorer.*

Leif Erikson lands in Newfoundland in 1000 A.D.

◂ *Leif Erikson, son of Erik the Red, followed in his father's footsteps and became an explorer.*

King Canute becomes ruler of England in 1015 A.D.

▴ *King Canute was the son of King Swein.*

# Viking Settlements

**During the Viking Age, a period that stretched from 787 A.D. to about 1000 A.D., the Vikings lived in Norway, Sweden, and Denmark, which make up the region of Scandinavia. These countries had little suitable land for farming, so the Vikings sailed the cold and stormy oceans in search of new lands to settle.**

## Glaciers and Mountains

In the northern parts of Norway and Sweden, mountains and **glaciers** covered the lands. Pine forests on the mountain slopes provided wood for building homes and ships. In the south, small amounts of flat land were suitable for growing food. The rivers that ran down the mountains were used to water crops. In Sweden, the Vikings had over 100,000 lakes full of freshwater fish for food. Fjords, or deep inlets of water, along the coastlines made perfect harbors for boats.

## A Flat and Fertile Land

Denmark was the smallest and southernmost Viking country. Its flat land was easily flooded when heavy rains caused the rivers to overflow their banks. Farmers grew wheat, barley, peas, turnips, and beans in soil made **fertile** by floodwaters. They also herded sheep and cattle and raised pigs. Wood for building homes and ships was gathered from the forests of oak and beech.

▼ *The Vikings sailed the Atlantic Ocean to explore and conquer many lands.*

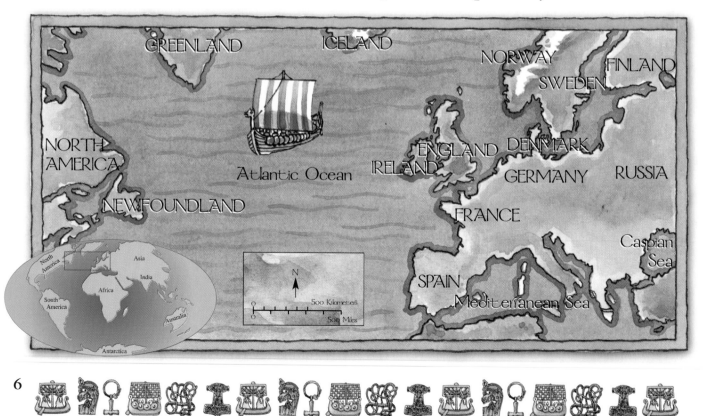

## A Hunt for New Lands

By about 800 A.D., the population of the Viking lands had grown so much that there was not enough land for every family to farm. Powerful landowners, called chieftains, gathered followers, or *hirds*, to help them take over their neighbors' lands. To increase their wealth, chieftains raided nearby countries, such as Ireland, England, and France to steal gold, silver, and other treasures. Over time, the Vikings began to settle permanently in some of the countries they raided. Viking settlers sailed to these countries in cargo ships, called *knarrs*. The *knarrs* carried the Vikings' families, their belongings, and their farm animals.

▲ *The Vikings sailed to many nearby countries in search of valuable land and treasures.*

▲ *The steam from Iceland's hot springs inspired the Vikings to call the area* **Reykjavik,** *meaning "bay of hot springs."* **Reykjavik** *is Iceland's capital city today.*

## Vikings in Ireland

Norwegian Vikings raided towns and villages on the coasts of Scotland and Ireland. They fought the Picts, the people who lived on the Orkney and Shetland Islands, north of Scotland. The Vikings destroyed Pict culture and built several settlements on the islands. In Ireland, the Vikings built a town that they used as a base for raiding nearby areas. This town became Dublin, Ireland's capital. By 840 A.D., Vikings had permanently settled in Ireland, where they traded cultural customs with the Irish.

## Land of Ice

Around 860 A.D., Naddodd, a Norwegian Viking, discovered a cold island covered with mountains. The island was Iceland, a land of glaciers, **geysers,** and boiling mud lakes created by underground **hot springs**. Ten thousand Norwegian Vikings lived on the island by 930 A.D.

## Erik the Red's Trick

Erik the Red was born in Iceland and is famous for discovering Greenland. In 982 A.D., Erik sailed westward after being **banished** from Iceland for three years for killing two neighbors during a quarrel. When Erik returned to Iceland, he announced that he had discovered a land of dense forests. He called this land Greenland to convince the Vikings to settle there, but most of it was arctic **tundra**, and the coastline was covered with enormous glaciers. Erik persuaded twenty-five boatloads of Vikings to sail to Greenland with him.

## Settling in Greenland

Although Greenland was not as pleasant as Erik had said, there was at least enough land for all the settlers to farm. Iceland had become overcrowded and **deforested**, so the settlers were not angry with Erik for his deception. The new settlers of Greenland fished and hunted polar bears, caribou, seals, and whales. They established a trade route to Norway, and traded salted fish and polar bear furs for tools, timber, and honey.

## A Great Discovery

In 1000 A.D., Erik's son, Leif Erikson, sailed from Greenland to explore farther west and discovered the island of Newfoundland, in Canada. Leif also found a forested land, which he named Vinland for the grapevines growing there. The Vikings tried to establish permanent bases there but were under constant attack by the **indigenous** peoples. The Vikings eventually abandoned their settlement and returned to Greenland. Europeans did not visit North America again for almost 500 years, until 1492.

▸ *Polar bear furs were trade items.*

▾ *Restored sod houses at the Viking settlement at L'Anse aux Meadows, Newfoundland, Canada.*

## The English Vikings

The Danish Vikings began to invade England after 850 A.D. because of the country's large amount of fertile farmland, dense forest, and supplies of copper and iron. After landing on the northeast coast of England, bands of Vikings on horseback rode across the country, attacking towns and cities as they went. They soon conquered all of the north and east of England. Eventually, Viking settlers developed the city of Jorvik into a major trading town.

# Russia's Name

When a Viking named Rurik settled in Eastern Europe, the local people called him *Rus*, which is the Slavic word for Viking. As his territory grew, the whole area became known as *Russia*.

▼ *The Viking warrior named Rurik.*

## Conquering the Slavs

When the Swedish Vikings wanted more land and new trade routes, they traveled eastward along rivers to what is now Russia. The area was the home of a group of farming people called the Slavs. Swedish Viking warriors invaded this land around 800 A.D., and made the Slavs build towns and roads, or sold them as slaves.

Russia had valuable natural resources. The Vikings trapped many native animals for their furs, such as bears, otters, and mink. The wide rivers allowed cargo ships to easily transport these prized furs and other trade goods.

## Raiding England

The first Viking raid on England was in 787 A.D. It took Vikings from Denmark less than a day to sail from Denmark to England. The Vikings attacked **monasteries** and churches for their silk cloth, and silver crosses and chalices, or drinking cups.

▲ *Viking ships traveled on Russia's wide rivers.*

# Viking Society

**The most powerful people in Viking countries were kings and chieftains, who controlled the land and owned slaves. Freemen owned small farms, or worked for a chieftain by farming on his land.**

## Kings and Chieftains

Viking kings were powerful leaders who ruled over Scandinavian lands. The lands were divided into territories controlled by chieftains. A Viking became a chieftain through his wealth, his skill in battle, and his ability to command respect from others. The more wealthy a chieftain was, the more followers he attracted. Chieftains increased their power by defeating other chieftains in battles over land.

## Feasts and Power

To keep their followers happy, chieftains held feasts in their halls and served plenty of meat, beer, and mead, an alcoholic drink made from honey. Horses were killed as a **sacrifice** to the Viking gods before being boiled and served to the guests. There was always music, singing, and storytelling at the feasts, and some historians believe that the Vikings sometimes wore animal masks during the entertainment.

Viking Social Pyramid

King

Chieftains and Warriors

Freemen

Slaves

▲ *Viking society was strictly organized. The king controlled the land and ruled over his people. Chieftains and warriors defended the land and conquered new land. Freemen and their families farmed and made goods. Slaves did the hardest work, such as collecting wood and building fences.*

## Freemen

Viking men who were not chieftains, warriors, or slaves were freemen. Most freemen were farmers. Some owned small farms, while others were allowed to live on and farm a chieftain's land. They paid the chieftain by working on his farm, building his ships, and melting iron to make weapons and tools. Some freemen were traders, traveling entertainers, or **artisans**, such as blacksmiths, who were paid by the chieftains to make jewelry, weapons, tools, and iron nails for shipbuilding.

## Viking Women

Viking girls were often married between the ages of twelve and fifteen to men chosen by their fathers. As wives, the girls spent their days spinning and weaving cloth from wool, brewing beer and mead, and cooking. Wives also had to look after their farms when their husbands were away. A Viking woman was allowed to divorce her husband if he mistreated or insulted her. She could not inherit property from her parents unless she had no brothers to whom it could go instead.

## Viking Slaves

Slaves, the lowest class in Viking society, were not free people. Some were people captured in Viking raids, and others were Vikings who had committed serious crimes, or had debts they could not pay. Each chieftain had about 30 slaves, and kings had more. Slaves had to obey their masters at all times and were often harshly treated. It was not a crime for a Viking to kill his own slave, but if he killed another Viking's slave, he had to pay for a new one.

◄ *Viking swords were made of iron or silver, and had names and designs carved into them.*

▲ *Children born to slave women became the property of the woman's owner.*

# Viking Surnames

**Each Viking child was given his or her father's name as a surname. If a Viking named Niels Larsen called his son Jens, Jens' surname would be Nielsen. The endings "sen" or "son" meant "son." The name Jens Neilson meant "Jens, son of Niel." A last name that ended in "datter" or "dotter" meant "daughter."**

# Daily Life

**Most Vikings lived on small farms in buildings called longhouses. Families of grandparents, parents, and children lived together in the same house, and everyone in the family worked on the farm. Wealthy families owned slaves to help with hard labor such as removing stones from the farmland.**

## Longhouses

Longhouses were made of blocks of sod, stone, and wood, if it was available. The roofs were thatched with straw, reeds, or **heather**. They were about 10 feet (3 meters) wide and 100 feet (30 meters) long, and usually consisted of one room with a central fire pit. Longhouses did not have windows, but a smoke hole in the roof let in light and fresh air.

Viking homes had little furniture. People sat on wooden benches packed with soil that lined the inside walls of the house. The benches were also used as beds and were covered with fur in wealthy households.

▶ *The Vikings lived in longhouses.*

## Farming and Fishing

Viking farms had a shed for storing food and larger farms also had a blacksmith's house and a slave hut. Farmers grew vegetables, such as onions, cabbages, and turnips, and grains, such as barley, wheat, and **flax**. They also kept pigs, cows, sheep, and geese on their farms. Horses were used for transportation, and to pull carts and plow fields.

From the oceans surrounding their homelands, the Vikings caught fish to eat. They also sailed further out into the Atlantic Ocean to fish for cod, haddock, and mackerel, and to hunt seals, whales, and walruses.

▲ *Women and children searched the coastlines near their homes for oysters.*

## Viking Meals

Vikings usually ate simple meals twice a day. Breakfast was often bread made of wheat, oats, or rye served with leftover meat. Dinner was either meat roasted on a spit, fish, or a stew of vegetables and meat, such as pork, beef, and mutton, or sheep.

## Viking Fashion

Most Viking clothing was made from wool. Men wore woolen trousers held up by a strap around the waist or long straps tied around the legs. They also wore woolen undershirts and long-sleeved tunics. Women wore long woolen dresses which they protected with aprons or overdresses. Woolen or fur cloaks kept Vikings warm in cold weather.

▸ *Viking clothes were made of wool or linen cloth, which was brightly colored using vegetable dyes. Their clothing was often embroidered, or decorated with colorful thread.*

## A Child's Life

Viking children began working when they were around five years old. Girls helped their mothers with weaving, cooking, and brewing beer and mead. The strongest girls were sometimes taught how to use weapons, such as knives, swords, and spears. Boys accompanied their parents as they worked on the farm to learn how to care for crops and animals. They were also taught how to fight with weapons, to **navigate**, and to build and repair ships. Some boys were sent to work as **apprentices** to blacksmiths or other artisans.

13

# Trading and Raiding

**Most early Vikings supported themselves and their families by farming and fishing. Through their travels, raids, and conquests, the Vikings gained huge wealth and became the greatest international traders of their time.**

## Trading Towns

The Vikings held small marketplaces and trade fairs in Scandinavia. Among themselves, the Vikings traded meat and salted fish, livestock, wine, woven cloth, jewelry, pottery, glass, weapons, and slaves.

As Viking trade increased, some Viking marketplaces grew into major trading centers. The largest ones were Birka in Sweden, Hedeby in Denmark, Dublin in Ireland, and Jorvik in England. The trading towns were located on the coasts or on rivers that Viking ships could easily sail to. Traders from as far away as China came to these towns to trade with the Vikings.

## Valuable Silver

Silver was one of the Vikings' most prized items. The Vikings in Russia set up a trade route that ran southward to Baghdad in modern-day Iraq. Viking goods, such as slaves, furs, and honey, were exchanged in Baghdad for silver coins, known as *dirhems*.

▲ *Vikings fastened their cloaks over one shoulder with silver brooches.*

▶ *Viking trade goods included tapestries, such as this one showing the Norse gods, Odin, Thor, and Frey.*

## Looking for Luxuries

The Vikings began to trade with other countries to supply their chieftains with luxury goods, such as silver jewelry. The chieftains used these items to flaunt their wealth and to reward their followers.

The Vikings traded leather, walrus **ivory**, slaves, and foods, such as grains for making beer and breads. Furs from bears, otters, foxes, and minks were also popular items for trade. In return for these goods, Vikings received silks from China, spices from India, wine from France, glass and pottery from Germany, and tin from England. Every year, Viking traders sailed on ships laden with cargo to the large trading cities of Rome and Constantinople, which is modern-day Istanbul, in Turkey.

▲ *The Vikings traveled far beyond Scandinavia's borders in search of new countries to raid. They sailed along the coasts, and took as many weapons, tools, clothing, jewelry, and slaves as they could.*

# Viking Coins

Early Vikings did not use coins to pay for goods. Instead, most used a system called barter, whereby a person exchanged goods or work for other goods that he or she wanted. Wealthy Vikings often paid for their goods with silver. Traders carried scales to weigh silver bars, coins, and jewelry because the value of the item was based on the weight of the silver in it. Once Vikings had settled in other lands, they made copies of those nations' coins to use.

## Christian Treasures

During Viking times, Christianity was the major religion of most European countries. This religion was based on the teachings of Jesus Christ, whom his followers believed was the son of God. As Christianity spread, many churches were built, and some men became **monks** and lived in monasteries. Foreign traders told the Vikings about the silver chalices, candlesticks, and statues inside the monasteries. Some chieftains saw their chance to gain riches, and gathered men in longships to raid the Christian monasteries.

## Surprise Raids

To carry out surprise attacks, Viking ships silently approached coasts at dawn. Before the local people had time to gather a defense force, the Vikings landed on the beach and stormed the church or monastery. After stealing treasures, such as silver chalices, silk cloth, and crucifixes, the Vikings sometimes burned the buildings down. If it was a long voyage back home, the Vikings raided the nearby towns for food. Anyone who resisted the Vikings was either killed or taken as a slave.

## The Raiding Season

The Vikings raided in spring and summer, after the crops were planted. Most Viking women stayed home to tend the farms, but some joined the raids. A woman warrior was usually the only child of a Viking couple. She wore the same clothing as men did while fighting.

◄ ► *The Vikings decorated the prows, or fronts of their ships, with carvings of dragons and various painted designs.*

## Attacks on Cities

With each success, the Vikings became bolder, traveling farther in their search for new conquests. They began to strike inland, rowing their ships up rivers to wealthy towns. In 843 A.D., the Vikings attacked the French city of Nantes, and in 859 A.D., they almost destroyed the city of Pisa, in Italy, before being driven out by the city's defenders.

## Battle Tactics

Once on land, Viking warriors stood shoulder to shoulder in rows, advancing against the enemy. Shields were held so that they overlapped and formed a wall that was difficult for the enemy to break. The warriors stabbed at the enemy with short spears and double-edged swords. Some warriors swung heavy iron battle-axes. If a Viking was killed, the shield wall broke down and the Vikings moved into smaller groups to fight. The Vikings despised cowardice and so always fought to the end. Their refusal to surrender meant that they sometimes won battles against much larger armies that had **archers** and **cavalry**.

## The Berserkers

The most fearsome Viking warriors were the berserkers. They went into battle wearing bearskins, believing that this gave them the strength of bears, and rubbed mixtures of chalk, charcoal, and egg yolk on their faces to make themselves look more terrifying. Before battle, berserkers worked themselves into an excited state by drinking a lot of mead and beer, and howling like animals.

## Paying to Be Left Alone

Viking attacks were so ferocious that other countries paid the Vikings to be left alone. The French gave the Vikings part of northern France, known today as Normandy, and paid them 700 pounds of silver every year. When the Vikings conquered most of northern and eastern England in 869 A.D., the territory became known as the Danelaw. The English paid the Vikings with Danegeld, or "tax paid to the Danes," to keep them from attacking farther south.

▲ *A shield helped protect a Viking in battle.*

▶ *The berserkers were fearless warriors.*

# Gods and Giants

**The early Vikings worshiped a number of gods and goddesses and believed in an afterlife where great warriors were rewarded. As the Vikings settled in new lands across Europe, they began to accept the beliefs of other peoples.**

## Nine Worlds

Vikings believed that the world of humans, which they called Midgard, or Middle Earth, was only one of nine worlds. The other worlds included Asgard, the home of the gods; Hel, the place of the dead; and Jotunheim, the land of the frost giants. Each world was believed to be at a different height on the trunk of a great ash tree, named Yggdrasil, which stretched up through the universe.

## Gods and Goddesses

Odin was the Vikings' supreme god of wisdom and warfare. The most popular god was Thor, the thunder god. He was believed to have worn a magic belt made by dwarves that gave him incredible strength, and to have hit giants with his hammer, without ever missing his mark. The most important female god was Freya, who was the goddess of love and fertility.

## Ragnarok

The Vikings believed that the end of the world would be caused by a severe ice age that would destroy human civilization. Odin would then lead the gods of Asgard in a final battle called Ragnarok, against the giants, led by the mischievous god, Loki. This fierce battle would destroy the universe, and the surviving gods would rule a new world.

*▲ This brooch shows the giant snake Jormungand, that Thor, the thunder god, fought in a battle.*

*◄ Odin was the ruler of the gods. He gave up one of his eyes in exchange for wisdom.*

## Life in Valhalla

Vikings believed in an afterlife, or a life after death. The souls of most people were thought to go to Hel, a place like Earth, where they would stay until Ragnarok. Evil people became ghosts, while warriors who died in battle were taken to Valhalla, Odin's hall. In Valhalla, warriors ate well, drank as much mead as they wanted, and practiced for war so that they could help the gods battle Loki and the giants at Ragnarok. Valhalla was believed to have more than 500 doors to accommodate all the Viking warriors who arrived after dying in battle.

▼ *The Vikings buried their dead in funeral ships with items to be used in the afterlife.*

▲ *Large stones were placed around Viking graves in the shape of a boat.*

## Funeral Ships

The Vikings buried their dead in ships as a symbol of the journey that the soul makes to the next world. Chieftains and warriors were often buried in large longships filled with items for the afterlife, such as weapons, clothing, jewelry, and horses. Ordinary people were buried in smaller boats and had fewer items buried with them. Sometimes a ship was burned, and its ashes buried in the belief that the dead person's spirit would be carried to the next world more quickly.

## The Coming of Christianity

The Vikings first encountered Christianity when they settled in Ireland, France, and England. The Viking settlers there became Christians in about 900 A.D. By 1100 A.D., Iceland and the Scandinavian countries had converted to Christianity, and Christianity was made the official religion of the Vikings. Even after becoming Christians, the Vikings did not abandon their beliefs in Norse gods. Amulets and gravestones often depicted both Christian and Norse symbols.

# Ruling the Land

**One of the Vikings' most important developments was their system of government. The Vikings had one of the earliest democratic societies, in which common people, not rulers, made laws.**

## Thing Meetings

The early Vikings met in outdoor assemblies, known as *things*. There, they settled disputes, passed laws, and judged crimes. Chieftains and land-owning freemen attended *things* to speak, debate, and vote. Men who did not own land, women, and slaves were not allowed to participate, but were sometimes allowed to attend the assembly. Every man attending a *thing* was expected to be peaceful and unarmed.

## Iceland's Parliament

In 930 A.D., Iceland created the *Althing*, the world's first **parliament**. Every summer, Iceland's chieftains met at Thingvellir, where a dip between the mountains made a natural **amphitheater**. Over a period of two weeks they passed laws, and resolved disputes that had not been settled at regional *things*. Every freeman was allowed to speak at Thingvellir if he wished.

▼ **Things** *were so important that freemen who owned land were fined if they did not attend.*

## Crime and Punishment

A victim of a crime or a member of the victim's family attended a *thing* to charge the person suspected of the crime. Twelve *thing* members then tried the accused. Anyone found guilty of a crime had to pay the victim or the victim's family. The amount depended on the seriousness of the crime. A person found guilty who did not pay the fine was banished from the community for a certain length of time. Murderers were banished for many years and were sometimes never allowed to return.

## Women and the Law

Women were not allowed to speak or vote at *things*, even if they owned land. If a woman was accused of a crime, a male family member spoke in her defense. If she was found guilty, her guardian, who might be her father or husband, was held responsible for her actions and had to pay a fine for her punishment.

▲ *(top left) A jewelry pendant marks the 1,000-year anniversary of* **Althing.**

▲ *(top) In Iceland, Viking chieftains held the* **Althing** *at Thingvellir during the summer.*

# Reading the Runes

**The Vikings called their language *donsk tunga*, which means "the Danish tongue." Today, it is known as Old Norse. Vikings of the Scandinavian countries spoke this language, but with slightly different dialects. Vikings wrote their language by carving into bone, wood, or stone.**

## Writing

The Vikings' alphabet consisted of runes. The rune letters were made up of straight lines, which made carving them easier. Runes were used to engrave owners' names on belongings, and makers' names on goods they produced. Viking warriors decorated their swords and spears with runic characters. Receipts for goods were carved onto sticks, as were notes that were sent by messenger.

## A Viking's Notebook

Historians believe that many Vikings could read and write runes. Children were also taught to read and write. Writing was practiced using a wooden tablet covered with melted wax. The wax was allowed to cool before being engraved with an iron knife or chisel to form the letters.

▲ *Viking writing tablets were 12 inches (30 centimeters) long with a raised wooden border.*

◄ *The most famous examples of Viking writing are on rune stones. The Vikings engraved and set up large stones as memorials to famous Vikings or loved ones. Many rune stones still stand in Scandinavia.*

## Stories and Poetry

Vikings were talented storytellers and poets. Their tales are of heroic warriors, brave sailors, and battles between gods and giants. None of these stories were written down on runes. Instead, they were spoken and passed down from generation to generation for hundreds of years. With Christianity came the Roman alphabet and the method of writing with ink on **parchment**. Around 1100 A.D., Icelandic poets and storytellers began to write down the stories and poems in the Icelandic language. Iceland's literature is the main written source of Viking stories.

▼ *Viking petroglyphs, or carvings or line drawings on rock, have been discovered in Scandinavia. A worker examines a Viking petroglyph depicting religious symbols.*

# Reading Runes

There were not enough runes to represent all of the sounds in the Old Norse language. This meant that a single rune could represent several sounds, making runic inscriptions difficult to translate. The first line of a rune was usually written from left to right, the second from right to left, and so on. Some rune stones had lines of writing that ran up and down.

▲ *The straight lines of Norse runes made them easier to carve.*

## Sagas and Storytellers

One of the most famous books in Icelandic literature is the *Prose Edda*, written by Snorri Sturluson around 1200 A.D. The book contains mythological stories of the Norse, or Viking gods, goddesses, giants, and dwarves. Icelanders also wrote family histories and sagas. *Heimskringla*, also written by Snorri Sturluson, is a history of Norway and the famous warriors who lived there.

Histories of heroic chieftains and tales of Norse gods and giants were spoken in verse to music and had riddles for the listeners to solve. Viking kings hired professional storytellers, called *skalds*, to make up poems about their bravery and skill in battle to recite at the royal court.

The Vikings filled the cold days of winter and early spring with many feasts and festivals. Viking gatherings included music, singing, and playing games. The Vikings also completed artwork, and many everyday items were decorated with intricate engravings or jewels.

## Musical Entertainment

The Vikings sang and played music at home, as well as at festivals, feasts, and funerals. Panpipes and hornpipes were made from cow horns or sheep bones. The Vikings also played lyres, which were similar to guitars, and rebecs, which were like violins. The strangest-looking musical instrument was the lur. This was a long cone-shaped wooden **wind instrument** that sounded like a deep trumpet.

## Activities

The Vikings participated in activities, such as sledding, skiing, and skating. These were also common forms of transportation in winter. Vikings enjoyed indoor activities, such as board games. One of the most popular board games was called *Hnefatafl*, meaning "knight's table." This game was very similar to modern chess, and was played in many countries throughout Europe.

▲ *A Viking ice skate was made of a leather shoe attached to a carved cattle bone.*

▶ *The Vikings carved musical instruments from wood, animal horns, and bones.*

## Decoration

Viking art was used to make everyday items look attractive. Dishes, pots, chests, and weapons such as shields were engraved with runes or painted with images of mythical beasts, gods, and warriors. A common Viking decoration was the gripping beast, believed to ward off evil. Long, thin creatures with tendrils were carved winding up and around an object.

▲ *Wooden Viking shields were painted with colorful designs.*

## Jewelry

Many Viking artisans were skilled engravers and jewelers. One of the most common types of jewelry made by Viking blacksmiths were arm or neck rings made of silver. Chieftains often had these rings made for themselves and their wives as a sign of wealth. Other jewelry was made of glass beads that were strung together. Many of the beads had yellow and black stripes, and were known as wasp beads. Metal jewelry was engraved with designs of interwoven curves and lines. Men wore silver pendants of Thor's hammer, which were thought to protect sailors against drowning and danger.

▶ **Hnefatafl** *game pieces were made of antler, bone, clay, stone, glass, or wood.*

# Viking Longships

The Vikings were expert ship builders, sailors, and navigators. They sailed the open sea between Scandinavia and North America in thin, fast ships called longships. The ships sailed easily into narrow ocean inlets and up rivers.

1. Thin, light, wooden planks were made by splitting tree trunks.

2. The strongest parts of the ship, such as the keel, were carved from branches, trunks, and sometimes the roots of oak trees.

3. The planks overlapped slightly and were fastened with iron nails. Fur or wool covered with tar was wedged between the wooden planks to keep the ship watertight.

4. The figurehead, which was a carved decoration on the prow, or front of the boat, was removed in open seas to prevent it from being lost. The figurehead was usually a carving of a dragon or snake.

5. Viking sails were square and made of woven wool colored in a striped or checkerboard pattern. The sail could be raised or lowered very quickly.

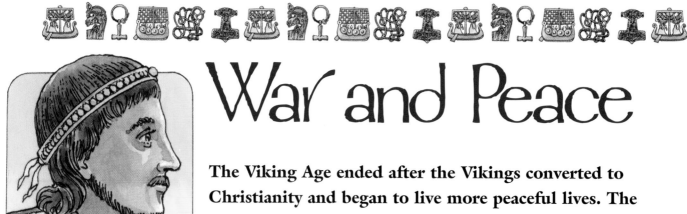

# War and Peace

**The Viking Age ended after the Vikings converted to Christianity and began to live more peaceful lives. The Vikings in England, Ireland, and France eventually married into local families and learned their culture. Russian Vikings married into Slav families and adopted Slavic customs.**

## Harald Bluetooth

After the Danish Viking king, Harald Bluetooth, converted to Christianity in 960 A.D., he decided to make Christianity the official religion of Denmark, and **persecuted** any Vikings in his country who did not convert. By 980 A.D., Danish Vikings, unhappy with the king's treatment, rebelled and began to raid England again.

## Viking Rule in England

One of the most fearsome Viking raiders was Swein, Harald Bluetooth's son. In 988 A.D., Swein forced his father from the throne and became the king of Denmark. His armies continued to raid the south of England. The young king of England, Ethelred, was so afraid of Swein and his army that he fled to France. In Ethelred's absence, Swein was not challenged when he came to England and claimed the throne in 1014 A.D.

## King Canute

With England under Viking rule, the Danish raids stopped. King Swein died unexpectedly in 1015 A.D. and his son Canute took over the thrones of England and Denmark. He ruled for the next 20 years. Gradually, the Vikings' culture in England became mixed with that of other peoples living in the area.

▲ *The Vikings established settlements in the new lands they conquered.*

▲ *(top) King Canute ruled the Viking countries of England and Denmark from 1015 A.D. until his death in 1035 A.D.*

## Rivals for the Throne

After Canute's death, the throne of England passed first to his son, Harold Harefoot, then to his other son, Hardicanute. Edward, Ethelred's son, took the throne in 1042 A.D. When he died in 1066 A.D., he had no **heir**. A **council** met and decided to make Earl Harold of Wessex, the most powerful man in England, the new king. He was crowned King Harold II in 1066 A.D. Duke William of Normandy, a relative of King Edward, and King Harald Hardrada of Denmark, a relative of King Canute, both claimed they should be king.

## A Double Invasion

In 1066 A.D., King Harald Hardrada invaded England with a Viking army of 10,000 men. The army, beaten by Harold's forces, retreated in chaos. It was the last time that Vikings threatened England. King Harold did not have time to celebrate his victory. Hearing that Duke William of Normandy was landing an army in the south of England, he set off for battle again. This time, King Harold lost. Duke William, later known as William the Conqueror, was crowned king of England. Norman kings, the **descendants** of Vikings, now ruled England.

▶ *The Mongols were fierce horsemen.*

## Genghis Khan Invades Russia

As the Vikings settled in Europe, a group of nomadic warriors from Mongolia called the Mongols attacked Russia. Under the leadership of Genghis Khan, the Mongols spread across Asia, creating an empire that stretched from China to Germany. In 1240, the Mongols attacked Kiev, and almost burned it to the ground. Russia came under Mongol rule and ended the age of the Vikings there.

## The End of Viking Greenland

The Vikings in Greenland lived quietly until the 1400s, when they suddenly disappeared. Historians do not know why, but some believe the disappearance was due to the **Inuit** peoples moving south from the Arctic and competing for territory.

▲ *William the Conqueror was a Viking descendant.*

# The Vikings Live On

**The Viking Age ended about 1,000 years ago, but the Vikings have not been forgotten. Their lives of adventure, travel, and trade are recalled in the words we use, in entertainment, in the history of several of the world's greatest cities, and in our government and legal systems.**

## Iceland's Heritage

Some of the Vikings' most long-lasting influences are found in Iceland. The people living there today are mainly the descendants of the Norwegian Viking settlers. The old Viking religion of many gods and goddesses is still one of several official religions in Iceland, where it is known as *Asatru*, and the parliament there is still called the *Althing*.

*▼ A Viking longship is burned during Scotland's Hogmanay, or New Year, celebration. During Hogmanay, thousands of people dress as Vikings from the Shetland Islands.*

*◄ The Vikings founded Dublin, the capital city of Ireland, more than 1,000 years ago.*

## Place Names

Place names of many European countries reflect their Viking past. The Viking territory of Normandy, France, retains its name, which means "Land of the Northmen." In England, many towns have names ending in "by" or "thorpe," which are Viking words for towns and villages. These towns were built on the sites founded by Viking invaders. Greenland has also kept the name given to it by Erik the Red.

## Courts of Law

The word for a local law, "bylaw," comes from the Viking words "by," and "law." During the Viking Age, twelve freemen tried a person accused of a crime. Today, law courts in many countries continue to use this Viking tradition. For some types of crime, the accused can choose to be tried by twelve members of a jury made up of members of the local community, rather than by a judge.

# Viking Artifacts

The best-preserved Viking remains have been found at burial sites. These sites allow archaeologists to learn what life was like during the Viking Age. Inside a burial mound in Norway, archaeologists found a ship built around 900 A.D. that contained the body of a Viking chieftain or king. The skeleton wore wool and silk clothing and was lying on the remains of a wooden bed. Fish hooks, cups, wooden plates and mixing bowls, and a large cask for holding water were also found on the ship. The bodies of twelve horses and six dogs were laid around the boat. The Vikings believed the chieftain would use all of these items in the afterlife.

*▼ Many silver Viking artifacts, such as arm rings, have been found in Ireland.*

# Glossary

**amphitheater** An open space or building with rows of seats rising gradually around a stage

**apprentice** A person who learns a trade by working with someone who is more experienced

**archaeologist** A person who studies the past by looking at buildings and artifacts

**archer** A soldier trained to use a bow and arrow

**artisan** A person who has skill in making a particular product, such as pottery or jewelry

**banished** Forced to leave a country or place

**cavalry** Soldiers who fight on horseback

**council** A group of people called together to make decisions or to provide advice

**deforest** To cut down and remove trees

**descendant** A person who can trace his or her family roots to a certain family group

**dialect** A version of a language that is used in a particular part of a country

**fertile** Able to produce abundant crops or vegetation

**flax** A plant used to make cloth, oil, and animal feed

**geysers** A natural flow of water from the ground that spews hot water and steam

**glacier** A large amount of ice and snow that builds up and slowly spreads over an area of land

**heather** A low-growing plant with pinkish-purple flowers

**heir** A person who receives money or property after someone's death

**hot spring** A flow of hot water from the ground

**indigenous** Native to an area

**Inuit** A member of a group of indigenous peoples living in the northern regions of North America

**ivory** A white, bone-like substance from the tusks of animals, such as elephants and walruses

**keel** The main piece of wood or metal that extends along the bottom of a boat

**monastery** A building where monks live and work according to strict religious rules

**monk** A member of a male religious community who has taken vows, such as silence or poverty

**navigate** To plan and control the direction of a ship or aircraft

**parchment** The skin of a goat or sheep that is prepared as a material to write on

**parliament** An elected governmental body that makes the laws for a country

**persecute** To cause suffering to others because of their beliefs, religion, or race

**sacrifice** An offering to a god or a goddess

**tundra** A large, treeless area of land found in cold, northern climates

**wind instrument** A musical instrument that is sounded by the player's breath, such as a horn

# Index

1 2 3 4 5 6 7 8 9 0  Printed in the U.S.A.  4 3 2 1 0 9 8 7 6 5